Copyright © 2018 by Boris "Bluz" Rogers
All rights reserved.
Published in the United States of America.
First edition.

No part of this book may be reproduced or transmitted in any form, or by any means, electronic or mechanical, including photocopying, recording or by any information storage or retrieval system without written permission from the publisher.

Obscure Popularity
HPJ Writeeasy Publishing
ISBN (Trade pbk.)
ISBN # 978-1-7330502-4-1
Layout and Design: Dasan Ahanu
Cover Art: Anthony Rodriguez

HPJ Writeeasy Publishing
Durham, NC

Obscure Popularity

Table of Contents

Good Karma	1
Miracle and Magic	2
Us Be	6
Rocket Science	8
The Get Back	9
Turn Down for What?	13
When They Come for You	16
Mike	18
Teddy P Jam	20
This Poem	22
Burial	26
The Sound of Trees	28

Good Karma

We all vibrate
Different
The difference is that some of us
Don't vibrate enough
Don't let our souls hum
Don't let our hearts knock
   Rock to a cosmic thump
Don't listen to universe when it speaks
But some of it be good karma
Be looking for
Something free
Something right
Something that feels like freedom
I mean we all looking to vibrate something positive while we live and breathe
   Do something good
Leave some beautiful karma for other souls to follow
A lil something righteous
To light up the darkness
Cuz we all burning bright
   We are all love and light
So breathe easy
And be
Good Karma

Miracle and Magic

there was a time in my youth,
some place, knee deep in my enormous innocence
that i knew dragons were real
    as hell
and i thought. No
    i knew that planes made clouds
how the poofy white smoke would spout out of the jet engine
like some Dr Seuss cloud-a-matic invention
flown by two kids
    that looked like me
except that story they might be white and from Whoville or what town or someplace city
but for a time in my mind that was the truth
like miracles
like magic

like myths
like fairytales
like children

when you were born
those dragons turned to steel
planes littered the sky with smoke lines
leaving evidence of their departure or destination
    on sunny days
clear days
you could find a patch of the coolest green grass
    lay on your back, track their paths
make a wish to be in a first-class seat to go wherever they're going
or to leave whatever they're running from
seemed easy
to do
because when you were born planes were everywhere
as abundant as birds, steel grace
metal defying its weight and deciding to fly
it's a marvel and if weren't for the science of it all
you would say it was a miracle or even magic

like you, when you were born
i looked at you with complete love and panic and
thought what have i gotten myself into
who are you, what a little strange stranger you are
you should have a name,
and i silently asked well, what did God call you
clearly cliche
thinking you must be one of his angels
gifted from heaven, so he had to call you something blah blah blah
at the time, i was so high off the feeling of being a father for the first time
that i was saying some real poety shit
but then the reality set in
this kid was mine, like for real
this miracle, marvel of magic
was depending on me to get my shit together
and I did, I got a job teaching kids
reading writing arithmetic
    that's what old folks call math
numbers
digits
 addition
    subtraction
        and the like
and for the first 6 days i was like
    "this being dad thing is cool"
i had a bunch of plans of things i would teach you
like how to ride a bike, tie a shoe,
    how to properly make a righteous fist to fight injustice or
    punch a boy in the face if you needed to
you know things a lil girl would need
or at least as a much as an overprotective father could conceive
but on day 7
on a clear day, a sunny day
a few air traffic controllers, and several hundred new yorkers
traced the path of a plane
    right into a building
it was not miracle, it was not magic
it was metal remembering its weight and destruction

it thirst for speed and violence
reminding us that it was not meant to fly,
as if it were angry at our audacity
    to believe we could be a part of the sky
we were reminded that we are fragile little humans
some of us passionate and pissed enough to fly planes into buildings
    i was reminded
on day 7 after you were born
heaven was going to be collecting
for your arrival,
it was as if God gave you to me but I didn't read the fine print
so little angel,
    little whatever your real name is
i know that there were days when planes left our sky blank and silent
as the day Picasso or Native Americans remembered it
before they decided to paint it on a wall of earth or canvas
those were days i canvassed the sky and searched for noise
for miracle or magic
for the lines, the evidence of departure and destination
written for small fingers to trace
but there was no trace,
no place in sky to say a plane had flown there
but I'm sure whispers of angel wings were everywhere
if we could only have been without enough sin
to see it
instead of wondering which kind of suicide those trapped in the building had to decide to go thru with
either to burn alive or try to fly...
hoping God would trace a path back to heaven
after the dive, maybe they closed their eyes
and just before the kiss of concrete
they would be snatched out of their bodies
    like miracle or magic
when u were born sept 4th
i believed in both
i believed God was a great magician
master of the sleight of hand

had me so focused on your birth that i would never see death slip
in
on a clear day, a sunny day
i'm reminded of the give and take of this life
the snatch and grab
the sun and moon in combat with the clouds and stars
for position in an empty sky
looking to be noticed or wished on
or believed in like magic or miracle
you are what I believe in
planes loaded with God are now myth
steel dragons from a fairytale
or a 9-11 bedtime story
that starts out with
when you were born
planes litter the sky like dragons and fireflies
like myth and magic

Us Be

you, sunset
me, dark horizon
us be a dawn
a slow warm rising
to a hard orange
soft yellow
exit to a bright sky blue

you, coke
me, an aged Hennessy
us be an expensive drink
sipped slow from glass
crafted by the hands of man who has never known the taste of either
us be rarity
us be cool
you, beautiful bass line
me, a smooth melody in the key of easy
us be a classic song
an orchestra, a blues song in a juke joint or a gospel choir
us be a fire

you, fist fight
me, no mercy
us be a gorgeous brawl
beautiful bruises from love taps
scrapping between sheets until we stain them ecstasy
until we crack ourselves in two
you distance
me regretted mistake
us be hard to fix sometimes
when we use words to break
to wage war with mouths
I shatter you into fragments

you, text message
me, apology letter too long to read
too complex to sort out

you, misunderstood prom queen
me, awkward freshman
us be a high school musical with fairytale ending
you, sugar
me, kool aid
us be summertime throwback love
family reunion bbqs,
    drunk uncle bad dancing to good music
us be the reason for existence, us be good loving
you, are God's Gospel gorgeous
me, a deep scar across the face
but us be picture perfect,
    framed for a supreme love affair
set up as pawns in heavens master plan
us couldn't plan to be in love no better
us be forever
us be something timeless
the first thing heard when first love was met
us be a Hip Hop heartbeat
house party red light basement groove
sometime us be ill communication
lost in arguments and translation
but decipher our meaning through our eyes
us be mo better blues sometimes
a good spike lee movie curled up on couch
    waiting for the message
sometime the message is so easy
as us, us be so easy
you are breath on my chest
i am fingers through your hair
us be forever, right here
sometimes

Rocket Science

You are rocket science
An impossible enigma of possibility

Folded up into strange origami
You are a 10th grade math problem
Hurting my 5th grade brain

A dividend invading my imagination
Like an army hell bent on occupying my time
I surrender every second to you
I white flag this fight to deny you
You are breaking news
Literally breaking me in two
With news of you

You are drama
A low speed chase on the 405
  I am Al Cowlinging it by your side
With people holding signs
  cheering us on
We are an outlaw love
The glove fits us
Skip the lawyers
Convict us
We did it
And will do it again, given the chance

You are impossible
I am stubborn

And this might work
If we shoot the for the moon
Once I figure out the rocket science of you

The Get Back

Get up black man
They gone think you dead lying there like that
They gone think you gave up
Stop fighting
This is the compliant they want for you
No pulse and silent

Get on your feet black boy
Stop laying there
like you got a bullet buried in your body
like the coroner is your Uber driver
with a free ride
ready to drive your body down to county

Hey black girl
Quit lying face down on the concrete
They gone think you stopped breathing
Gonna think you opened your body up for the beating
Like they nightsticks and fists
are a new shade of eyeshadow and lipstick
that you wanted applied to your face

Get off that ground little brother
They might mistake you as a job well done

As paid leave
As a retirement bonus
As accomplishment and accommodation
     placed in a coffin

Get on your feet black man black woman
     If you lay there too long
they will hashtag you
Place your face on white t-shirts looking like cotton tombstones

Get off the church floor black folk
They gone think you waiting on a resurrection
     waiting to be risen

waiting in a burger king line while you waiting to go to prison

On your feet Tamir rice
This playground is no place for children to die

On your feet Sandra Bland
You have no business dying in a jail cell

Rise up Eric Garner,
Rise up Keith Lamont Scott,
Rise up Philando Castile
Rise up Jonathan Ferrell

There are women and children waiting for you come home and protect them

On your feet Oscar Grant, Quan Brown, and Aaron Winchester
    Remind the bullet in your spine
how your ancestors gave you the birthright of back bone bravery

Get off the ground black woman
They gone think you ready for the grave
Think you got what you deserve cuz you aint know
    how to behave
Didn't cower in fear like they wanted you to

Get up off that ground before they put that media spin on you
Do a background check on you
Turn you into gangbanger monster
15 felony strikes on you
Turn you into a goon and drug peddler
A death dealer

    Turn your book into a gun
Your toy into a gun
Your wallet into a gun
Your CDs into a gun, your loose cigarettes into a gun
Your vernacular into a gun, your hands up on Oklahoma
highway into a gun
your mind into a gun

Your skin tone into a gun

You are a gun, they are scared of you so they shoot because you look like
a weapon,
      Like you dangerous, like a bad dude
Like Korryn Gaines, like Ayanna sleeping on her grandmother's couch

You look like a target that should be taken by deadly force
So get up off that ground
you ghosts of gone too soon.

We will not let you fall silently to their gunfire
We will not be quiet about your departure
Your unethical earthly eviction

Stop lying there waiting for them
to collect what they kill
And leave us to bury the remains

We don't get that back
We don't get that 40 acres and mule
That slave ship ride
Those black women who died
Suicided with baby by side
We don't get that back
We don't get back that picked cotton
Those callused hands
Sliced fingers
We don't get back our leaders
We don't get Our Kings, Xs and Evers back

Tamir Rice's mother doesn't get that back
Oscar Grant's mother doesn't get that back
Trayvon's Mom doesn't get that back

bitch I will write you under a house
That Dorothy built
That Dorothy crash landed

12

Loud Music for black boys to die to(for)(with)   turn down? for what?

In the beginning they wanted you silent
they wanted you silent
but
when you were born
your skin became a soundtrack
Background music to our history
An old slave's new freedom song
A civil rights march sung in the tune of we shall overcome
The funk of a blaxploitation flick
A rhythm in your boom box of a chest
created a movement
When you were born
you were born   LOUD
God composed you with jazz hands
Thru big band theory
Big banged you out on beat machine
You are a black Beethoven
walking this world with J Dilla
dripping thru your veins
your genius
Herbie Hancocked back
ready to blast shots of righteous soul
Howling wolf wailing from your gut
Hendrix in your liver
Prince and Otis Redding in full concert on your chin
An Earth Wind and Fire in your lungs
There's blues in your bones boy
Gospel in your laughter

Turn down? for what?

Because the music in you scares them
Scares them enough
 to pump bullets into your vehicle
At a gas station

On the day a Michael Dunn

pulls a gun on you for how loud your skin sounded
Barely hearing his own ignorance and fear
over the cranked-up decibels of God
rockin thru your body

Tell me what song were your eyes playing

What radio station was your smile tuned to Black boy

It must have been a proud one
It must have been heaven
   and you were the 7th caller
Cuz u won
Grand prize: called home

You and Trayvon were playing the same theme songs
that black boys seem die to

Turn down? for what?

So they can forget how beautiful you sounded
How hard the fight in your voice
echoed against this society
that stereotypically views you by the millions on YouTube
Views you best as a problem solved
by pretending you, your rights, and your justice don't exist
The close of your casket
is deafening
Your death will never be BDS coded
So it won't be on the radio
But your murder will always be requested

Their fear has become music for black boys to die to
Sounds like it got prison bars to rhyme thru
Like it got a shoddy record deal of a court appointed lawyer and got screwed
Can't pump up the jam like we used to
Too busy ducking down and dodging bullets aimed at you

This caliber of music they creating for black boys to dance to is dangerous
It won a Grammy for selling so much hysteria
   Track produced by Jim Crow America

They threw us a holy mackerel of a Macklemore MC
A Hip Hop red herring
to distract you from hearing
that America
still has black youth dying
The sound of them falling was so turnt up
The sound of mothers crying was so turnt up
that eardrums ruptured and the sound of hope
started fading into white noise

Black boys they are trying to silence you
one injustice at a time

Trying to mute your soul symphony
pull the plug
and snatch the electricity on your block party of a life
But I want you to never forget the volume of your greatness
How scared they are of how big you sound
and when they ask you turn your soul down
let them hear how your spirit gets crunk
Just open up your mouth and let the sound of God pour out
and tell em
Turn down? for what?

When They Come for You

When they come for you
they won't have their guns drawn
confidently etched out from their cold holsters
They now know
that the world is photoshoot ready
to digitally document their death squad tactics
That their antics
are now archived video clipped and Facebook status
set to go viral

even though our protest and proof are never enough fire to burn their house to ash
Our death
sometimes pins medals on their chest
and allows them to retire with sizable paycheck
But nonetheless,
we fight back best we can
So understand that now when they come for you
they startin at the foundation,
at your doorstep
They will be dressed as developer or realtor or hipster
Your best 90s Hip Hop bumping from their boombox
On your block
dressed in your latest fashion
appropriately appropriating your culture til they fit in,
till they move in
   Then the police traffic rises
      Crime seems to drop
Property tax rises around big mama old house
So much that her fixed income ain't enough income
   Now she forced to move out of the house she lived in for last 30 years
Done raised 2 generations of kids under that roof,
   but it is what it is aint it?
The neighborhood got more Volvos
And less Chevys candy coated painted
Because now…
    now your street is charming
Alarming ain't it?
The sound of your neighbors being shipped out
Handed hollow vouchers to move to a place unfamiliar
This be new Slave ship
Visit the new cool kids on the block
Tell them the story of the haunted trap house
where the ghost of dope boys still shed tears
You tried to get the city to tear down that nightmare for 3 years
After seeing the deferred dreams of high school hopes sit on its porch
waiting to snatch the soul from whoever walked by
Still Looking for a way out of this neighborhood

The same neighborhood that holds the street corner
The same corner your cousin died on
They re-paved and renamed it something expensive
Something you can barely afford to stand on
The block don't feel like it used to
Now the folks next door call cops on you
when your friends come thru
Strange how thangs done changed around you
This is progress
When they come for you
    they will say it's for the best
To clean up the mess
They call it restoration
Wanna free you from the mortgage or that rent and give you a new destination
They sellin false emancipation
Wanna reshape your school
and call it re-education
They will add a new word to your vocabulary
young blood
It's called
gentrification

Mike

You bittersweet moonwalk
Tan Peter pan
Neverland ranch
Grown man
With the ambitions of a 10-year-old boy
Wanting to own a carnival
And rights to the Beatles
You Bad
Like 50 zippers on a leather jacket
Like a gang fight
With nothing but dance moves
Like words that weren't words
They were mantras for us to march to
Mama say mama say amakusa

You Right hand disco ball
You are crotch grab
Choreographed
Blood on the dance floor
A smooth criminal
Leaning with
Gary, Indiana on his back
You were questioned
But could not question your greatness
Cuz the answer was always
Tell em that it's human nature
Why why

You live TV Lisa Marie Presley kissing
King of Pop...
Never needing the permission of the king
To Heartbreak his daughter
Pepsi Cola burn survivor
Jehovah witness turned
Werewolf turned zombie
Turned Ola Ray into
Wall posters and
Every preteen boy's wet dream
You and sister scream
While you got all the pretty young things
To repeater after me
Sayin naw naw naw

You concert sellout on global scale
Having grown men and women pass out
From the sheer sight of your stature
A Scarecrow easing on down the road
Reminding the man in the mirror
That the child in all of us
Still has a dream to chase
A rainbow to ride
Elephant man bones to purchase
A world to save
A childhood to never grow up from

That as adults we live and leave our lives
Pinned up against walls
Left to collect dust on shelves
We live our lives as shells of former selves
Instead taking the chance and liberating
Our own happiness
So tonight
You gotta leave that nine to five up on the shelf
Let the madness and music find a place in your bones
Then you go and find a place in this world
That looks and feels like a dance floor
And start living
Off the wall

Teddy P Jam

lets get outta here
lets get some place so far gone
gps can't find us
where us is the destination
our bodies laying in such a position that whoever was to witness us sinning
would be wishing to be in same position
or situation
I'm tired of waiting
putting on pounds with sweet thoughts of you
come on over to my place
let's unlace all the stress we've have tied up in old relationships
let's slip and fall into each other
no accident
no need for lawyer
let our ligaments get locked into lustful litigation
til our neighbors call for an objection to the noise of the heaven we making
the sensation of your taste
make me lose my place
my train of thought derailed without fail
i tailspin out of your beautiful sky
crash and sink in the sea between your thighs
i want you to come to my place tonight
so when i drive by wherever you are in the world tonight
get inside the ride and close the door

come in and close the door

you be the leading lady in every fantasy that my imagination can muster
you are solar flare in sundress
sometimes too bright to look at
i go blind staring at your gorgeous
mesmerized by the motion of your hips
when you walk across a room
it's on some Aaliyah fresh
i mean it's hard to believe you miss magnificence

it's the manifestation of black girl magic
beautiful voodoo
when you move the way you do
and when you speak
i forget to breathe
heart forgets to beat
you touch the skin on my cheek
and my epidermis is electrified as Frankenstein herself
has reconstructed the man inside
to remind me to love or at least live
and give you every part of me that hasn't already surrendered
to the almighty army of your heart and the kingdom in your eyes
so it's no surprise that you view me thru all my blues
every hue of my struggle
rainbows thru your peripheral
you see me...every crack and fissure
every mistake and mishap
every apology and every flaw
strip me down to my honesty now come in
close the door

This Poem

not this poem

this will not be the poem that storms the castle,
slays the three-headed dragon with nothing but my bare hands,
climbs the tower to lay a kiss on your lips,
to awake you from a long silent slumber
where after all these years your hair and face
   are still on fleek.

this will not be the poem
that promises you the moon and stars,
that promises you a life of unicorns and rainbows,
that has me spouting that you are my black queen,
   the essence of everything ebony,
mother of all things Afrocentric,
the center of our blackness.

no, this will not be that poem.

instead this will be the poem that will part the hair on your head,
slowly massage your scalp for 15 minutes
while you talk about how Dennis in accounting,
won't reimburse you for the money you spent
landing a client
for the company at some fancy restaurant.
   this nigga got you mixed up.

This will be the poem that will let you vent.

it will see the beauty in the weird way you eat
fried chicken.
it's a confessional booth.
it's the truth.
it's walking in the bathroom while you poop,
look you square in the face, taking a deep breath and say
"nigga…i love you."

this poem has no boundaries.

it's waking up with your morning breath and still wanting your sunrise sex.
this will be the poem that drives your momma around to every bath and body works in town
looking for moonlit path.

this poem will be our flesh and bones pressed together under sheets,
on a dance floor,
with scent of you two stepping in my nose.
this will be the poem that makes your clothes fall to the floor,
runs you a hot bath
so you can relax and
binge watch sitcoms on Netflix on the iPad.
this poem will not disturb you when you need
"me time."
not that you don't have me in mind it's just that sometimes
the solitude is the best thing for the mind.
this poem is unwinding.
it's me creeping up from behind while you do the dishes
   in a robe and house slippers
and it's about to go down
   right there
      in the kitchen.

listen,
this will be a poem about position.
all of them from bedroom to boardroom.
this poem will try to avoid boredom,
mundane same thang.
this poem is 4am
and me
nervous and sweaty with baseball bat in hand
investigating the house for the noise YOU heard
only to find nothing but the wind
that had tree branches rustling.
it's coming back to bed,
you rolling over saying "thank you"
and me saying

"you crazy! You woke me up and my adrenaline still pumping guess what,
we fucking!"

this poem is me sitting quietly
on Super Bowl Sunday
with your purse in my lap
while you rifle thru the clearance rack
trying on this and that
then turning to me and asking
"do i look fat?"
this poem won't answer loaded questions like that
it will lie to you if has to,

but understand that your confidence
will never be broken or fractured, no matter what my answer is.
your smile alone is a reminder that God created you beautiful.
your exquisiteness doesn't need
my confirmation or permission
to know how gorgeous you is.

this poem is no ego boost.
it's a reminder of how heaven you are
in sweatpants and granny panties,
old t-shirt and hair just
doin whatever a goddess's hair wants to do on a Sunday night.
this poem is normal...A.F.
it's waiting for you to get off work
so I can pick you up,
drive you home
to have dinner, watch the news
and if the mood and situation is right
we can turn off the lights and be sleep before 10 pm.

this poem is the sigh your grandfather heard ya grandmother make
when she was tired.
he knew in that one breath
that all she wanted him to was ask what's wrong
   not fix the problem,

        just listen.
this poem is all ears.
all shoulders to cry on.
it's anniversaries we forget sometimes
but make up the next day by sending way too many flowers to your job.
this poem is classic human.
bound to make mistakes,
   but make no mistake this poem is
     i love you.

Burial

at first you will deny the feeling
your manhood
will build a wall of epic ego
   beware this wall
it's hollow and easily toppled with a self-deprecating thought
or misplaced compliment

when the trophies become monumental mockeries
engraved with inside jokes of your greatness
when the world waits
   to claim its love and admiration for you
at your coma
        at your funeral
is when you understand
the feeling
has rooted itself
ready to grow strong

it wants you to water it with the clown tears
   and forced smile you wear in public
it will demand your sanity
        all of it
will sip it slowly with your depression and insomnia
until it is full and ready for the rest of you

there will be a hole somewhere in your chest
a void you try to fill with friends and busy work
with goals and dreams
with something that sounds like
joy
that echoes like
a smile
but still feels like the mirror calling you every derogatory name
it can think of
   Talk about stained glass

When your done with shell
don't leave it where your children can find it

That's not the memory you leave

But you will leave them

With questions
Anger, fear, frustration
The things that buried themselves inside
Called themselves a treasure for your children
to discover
When they turn your age
That's where they will find you
Inside them
Buried
deep

The Sound of Trees

if a tree falls in the woods does it make a sound?
interesting question
for years good minds have debated it
weigh it and measured it
hoping the answer would be found by some intellectual
scientific
and some of the greats go crazy from the sheer simplicity
of such a question
of course, if no one is there it still makes a sound
like a barky skyscraper screaming with the cracks of branches
on its way down
of course, if the tree falls or is taken there is a sound it's makin
as with all things taken
when nobody's lookin
like a child snatched from some park
or from their home
there is a sound there
it's called fear
like the sound of trees burning on hillside

the day Cecil the Lion died
it sounded
like an entire rainforest fell to an orchestra of angry chainsaws
like a million lumberjacks singin and swinging their lofty faith
with the deep gusty myth of Paul Bunyan
in their arms
hopin that each cut will fell the faith of every tree
and when they fall
they do make a sound
as loud as a lion's roar blended with the blast
of a hygienists high powered rifle
the bang
so big
the tree so tall
the fall
so
loud

www.ingramcontent.com/pod-product-compliance
Lightning Source LLC
LaVergne TN
LVHW051207080426
835508LV00021B/2848